Impressum
Verlag: BABADADA GmbH, Nedderfeld 112 , 22529 Hamburg
Geschäftsführer / Verlagsleitung: Harald Hof
Druck: Books on Demand GmbH, In de Tarpen 42, 22848 Norderstedt

Imprint
Publisher: BABADADA GmbH, Nedderfeld 112 , 22529 Hamburg, Germany
Managing Director / Publishing direction: Harald Hof
Print: Books on Demand GmbH, In de Tarpen 42, 22848 Norderstedt

school
ليكول

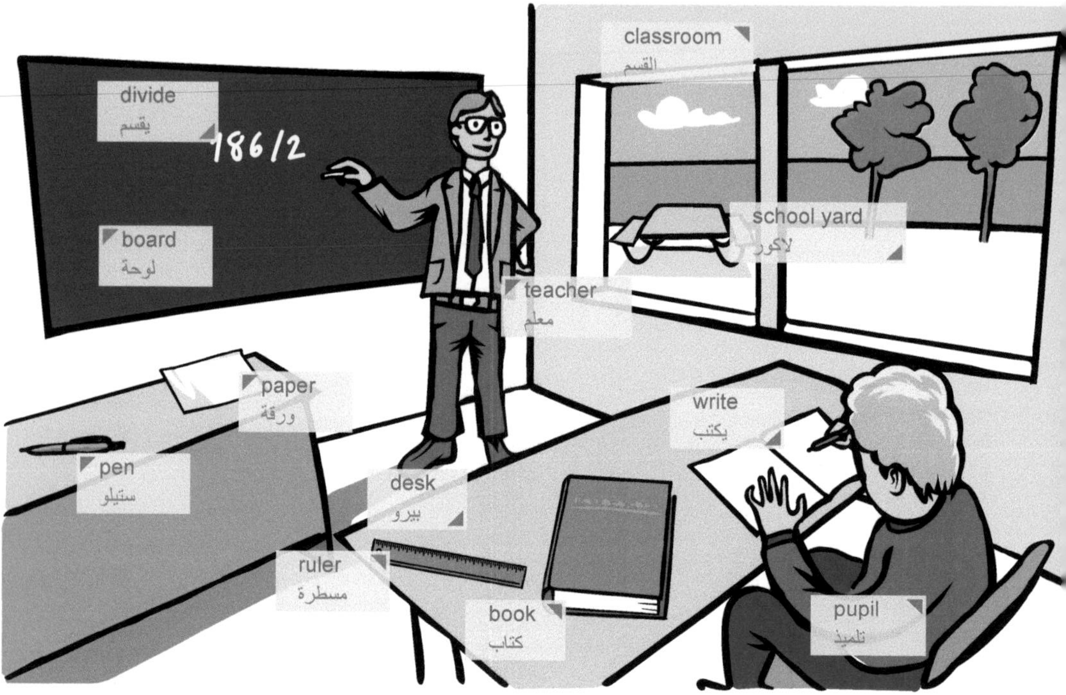
classroom
القسم
divide
يقسم
186/2
board
لوحة
school yard
لاكور
teacher
معلم
paper
ورقة
write
يكتب
pen
ستيلو
desk
بيرو
ruler
مسطرة
book
كتاب
pupil
تلميذ

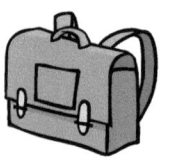

satchel

كرطاب

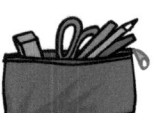

pencil case

المقلمة

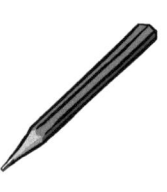

pencil

قلم الرصاص

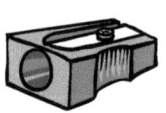

pencil sharpener

منجارة

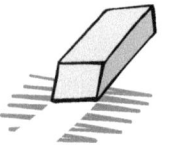

rubber

ممحا

drawing pad

الكايي تاع الرسم

drawing

الرسم

paintbrush

البانسو

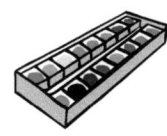

paint box

باتير

scissors

مقص

glue

كولا

exercise book

كايي تاع التمارين

homework

الواجبات

number

النيميرو

add

يجمع

subtract

يطرح

multiply

يضرب

calculate

يحسب

letter

الحرف

alphabet

الحروف

word

كلمة

text

النص

read

يقرا

chalk

طباشير

lesson

الدرس

register

دفتر المدرسي

exam

اماقزيل

certificate

سرتفيكا

school uniform

لوكيل تاع ةبللا

education

التعليم

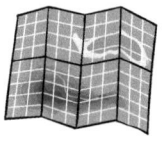

encyclopedia

كيبسكيل

university

الجاميعة

microscope

المجهر

map

الخريطة

waste-paper basket

بوبال

travel
فواياج

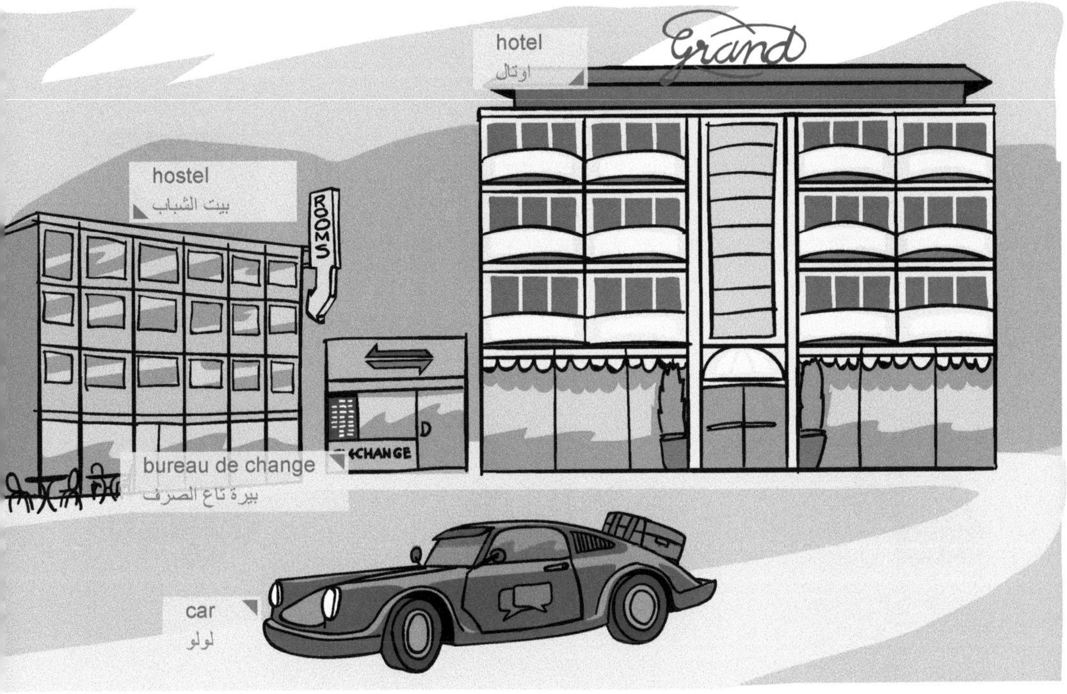
hotel
اوتال
Grand
hostel
بيت الشباب
ROOMS
EXCHANGE
bureau de change
بيرة تاع الصرف
car
لولو

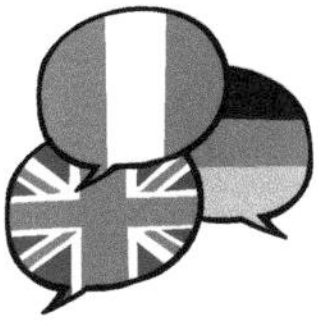

language

اللغة ليقصدها

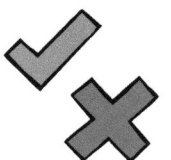

yes / no

واه / لا

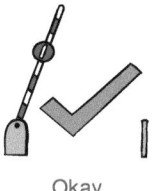

Okay

صحا

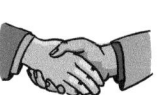

hello

مرحبا

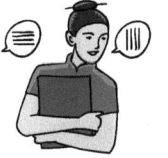

translator

طرجمان

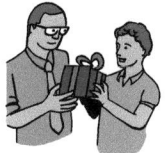

Thank you

صحيت

how much is...?

شحال السومة؟

I do not understand

مفهمتش

problem

مشكيلة

Good evening!

مسلخير

Good morning!

صباح لخير

Good night!

تصبح بخير

bye bye

بسلامة

direction

ديركسيو

luggage

الباقاج

bag

ساك

backpack

ساكادو

guest

ضيف

room

ثمبرا

sleeping bag

ساك تاع رقاد

tent

خيمة

tourist information

استعلامات سياحية

beach

بجر

credit card

كارطة ناع الكريدي

breakfast

فطور الصباح

lunch

الفطور

dinner

العشا

ticket

البيي

lift

اسونسير

stamp

تامبر

border

الحدود

customs

الديوانة

embassy

سقارة

visa

فيزا

passport

باسبور

transport

نقل

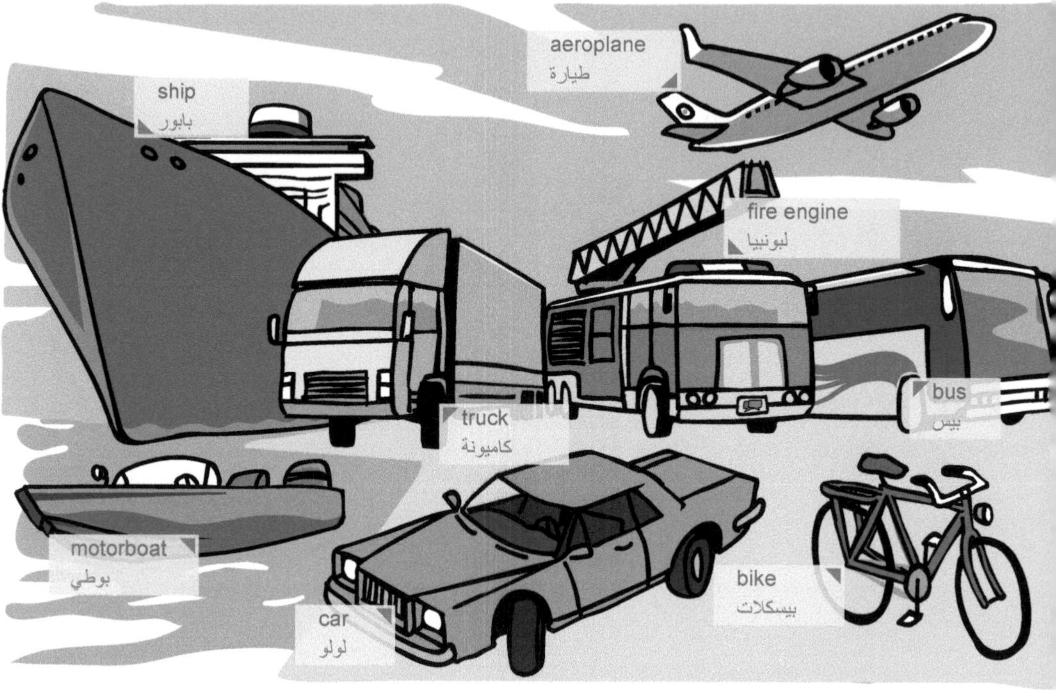
aeroplane
طيارة
ship
بابور
fire engine
لبونبيا
bus
بيس
truck
كاميونة
motorboat
بوطي
bike
بيسكلات
car
لولو

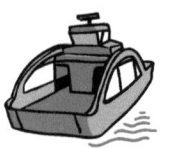

ferry

بابو

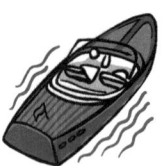

boat

بوطي

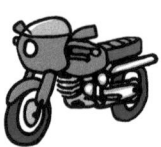

motorbike

موطو

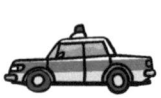

police car

لوطو تاع لابوليس

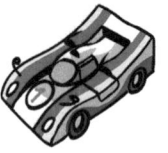

racing car

لوطو تاع السيباق

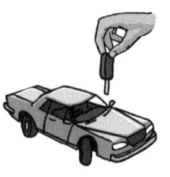

rental car

لوطو تاع كرية

car sharing

لواط اتاع كرية

breakdown truck

رومورك

refuse truck

كاميو تاع الزبل

motor

موتور

fuel

ليسونس

petrol station

ستاسيون

traffic sign

بانو

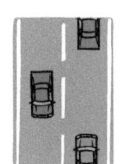

traffic

ترافيك

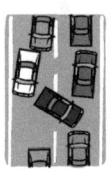

traffic jam

سركالة

car park

باركينغ

train station

لاقار

tracks

السبيكة

train

قطار

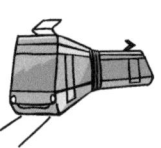

tram

ترام

carriage

فاغون

helicopter

اليكبتار

airport

مطار

tower

تور

passenger

مسافر

container

كونتنار

carton

كرطونة

cart

شاريو

basket

سلة

take off / land

يقلع / يهود

city

مان

village

قرية

city centre

البلاد

house

دار

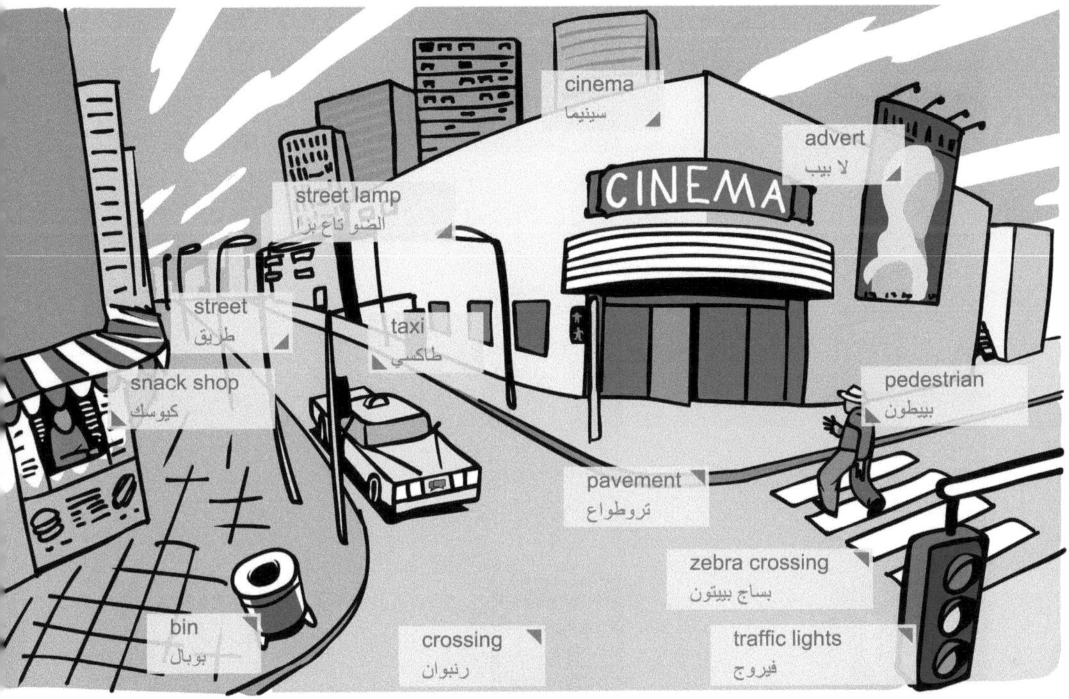

cinema سينيما

advert لا بيب

street lamp ابرا تاع الضو

CINEMA

street طريق

taxi طاكسي

snack shop كيوسك

pedestrian بييطون

pavement عاوطرو

zebra crossing بييتون ساجب

bin لابوي

crossing رنبوان

traffic lights فيروج

hut
كوخ

flat
برطمان

train station
لاقار

town hall
لاميري

museum
متحف

school
ليكول

university

الجامعة

bank

بانكة

hospital

سبيطار

hotel

اوتال

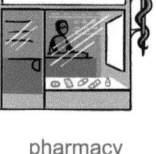

pharmacy

فارماسي

office

بيرو

book shop

مكتبة

shop

حانوت

florist's

فلوريست

supermarket

سوبرات

market

مرشي

department store

حانوت كبير

fishmonger's

مسمكة

shopping centre

سونتر كومرسيال

harbour

المينا

park

باراك

bench

بنك

bridge

جسر

stairs

درج

underground

ميترو

tunnel

تونال

bus stop

لاري تاع البيس

bar

بار

restaurant

مطعم

postbox

صندوق البريد

street sign

البانوات

parking meter

مقياس زمن الوقوف

zoo

حديقة حيوانات

swimming pool

بيسين

mosque

جامع

farm

فيرما

pollution

التلوث

graveyard

مقبرة

church

قليزية

playground

بارك

temple

معبد

landscape

الريف

signpost
بانو

way
طريق

meadow
مرج

stone
حجرة

tree
شجرة

hiker
رحالة

river
نهر

grass
حشيش

flower
زهرة

valley

واد

hill

جبل

lake

بحيرة

forest

غابة

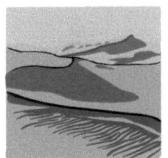

desert

صحرا

volcano

بركان

castle

شاطو

rainbow

قوس قزح

mushroom

فطر

palm tree

نخلة

mosquito

ناموسة

fly

ذبانة

ant

نملة

bee

نحلة

spider

رتيلة

beetle

خنفوس

frog

جرانة

squirrel

سنجاب

hedgehog

قنفود

hare

قنينة

owl

بومة

bird

زاوش

swan

بجعة

boar

حلوف

deer

عزالة

moose

إلكة

dam

سد

wind turbine

الطاحونة

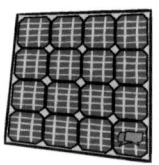

solar panel

خلية شمسية

climate

كليما

waiter
سارفور

menu
المونيو

chair
كرسي

soup
سوبة

pizza
بيتزا

cutlery
كوفار

tablecloth
ناب

starter

اوردوفر

main course

الطبق الرئيسي

dessert

ديسار

drinks

مشروبات

food

ماكلة

bottle

القرعة

fast food

فاست فود

street food

ماكلة نديه معايا

teapot

براد اتاي

sugar bowl

سكرية

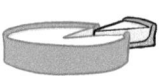

portion

طرف

espresso machine

ماشينة تاع اكسبريسو

high chair

كرسي عالي

bill

فاتورة

tray

سني

knife

خدمي

fork

فرشيطة

spoon

مغيرفة

teaspoon

مغيرفة تاع لاتاي

serviette

سربيتة تاع الطابلة

glass

كاس

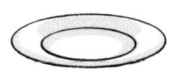

plate

طبسي

soup plate

بول

saucer

طبسي تاع الفنجال

sauce

لاصوص

salt pot

القوطي تاع الملح

pepper mill

طحان تاع الحرور

vinegar

خل

oil

زيت

spices

ليزيبيس

ketchup

كتشوب

mustard

موطارد

mayonnaise

مايونيز

supermarket

سوبرات

special offer
بروموسيو
customer
كلويون
dairy
مشتقات الحليب
fruit
فاكية
trolley
شاريو
FOR

BUTCHERS

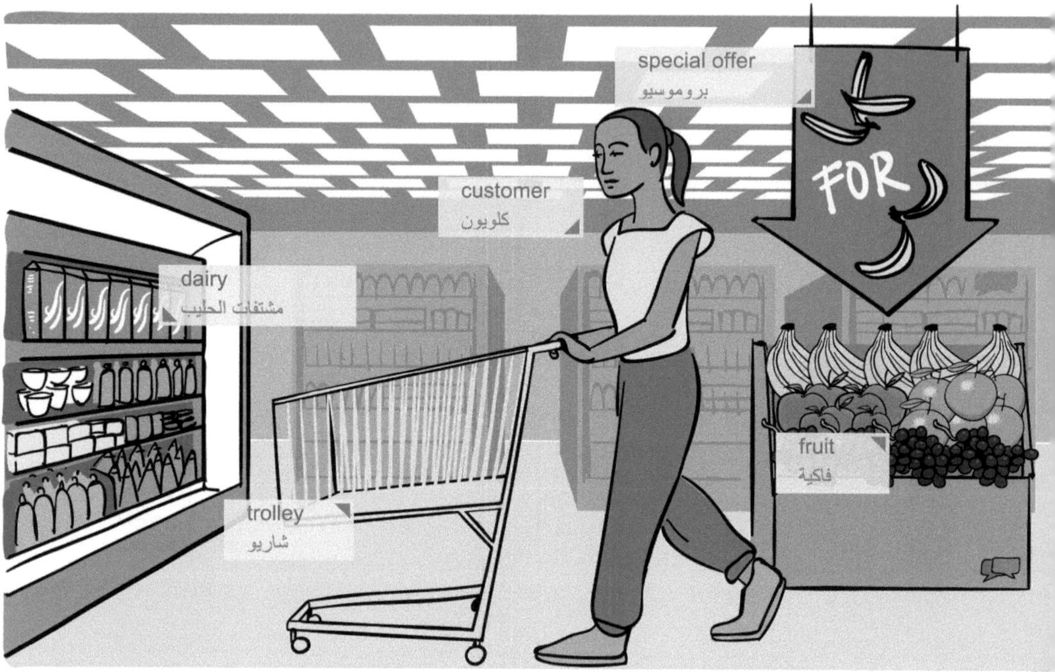

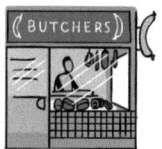

butcher´s

بوشي

BAKERY

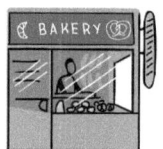

baker´s

بولونجي

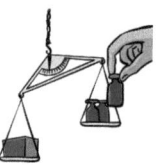

weigh

يوزن

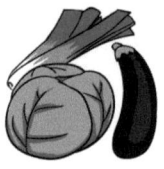

vegetables

خضار

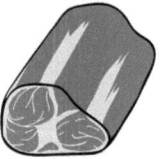

meat

لحم

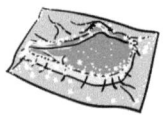

frozen food

سيرجولي

cold meat

كاشير

tinned food

كونسارف

washing powder

لغسيل تاع الوما

sweets

الحلويات

household products

صوالح الدار

cleaning products

ديتارجو

salesperson

فوندوز / خدامة فالحانوت

till

لاكاس

cashier

كاسسي

shopping list

ليستا تاع الشري

opening hours

سوايع الخدمة

wallet

متزدزت

credit card

كارطة ناع الكريدي

bag

ساك

plastic bag

بورصة

drinks

مشروبات

water

الما

juice

جو

milk

حليب

coke

كوكا

wine

الشراب

beer

البيرة

alcohol

شراب

cocoa

كاكاو

tea

لاتاي

coffee

قهوة

espresso

اكسبريسو

cappuccino

كابوتشينو

banana

بانانة

apple

تفاح

orange

تْشينا

melon

بطيخ

lemon

ليم

carrot

كروطة / زرودية

garlic

ثوم

bamboo

بانبو

onion

بصل

mushroom

شانبينيو

nuts

بندق

noodles

ليبات

spaghetti

سباقيتي

rice

روز

salad

سلاطة

chips

ليفريت

fried potatoes

ليفريت

pizza

بيتزا

hamburger

هانبورقر

sandwich

سندويش

cutlet

اسكالوب

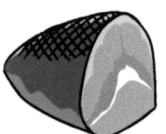

ham

لحم الحلوف

salami

سامي

sausage

مرقاز

chicken

جاجة

roast

لحم مشوي

fish

حوت

porridge oats

شوفان

muesli

موسلي

cornflakes

كورن فلكس

flour

فرينة

croissant

كرواسون

bread roll

خبيزة

bread

الخبز / كسرة

toast

خبز محمر

biscuits

بيسكوي

butter

زبدة

curd

لبن

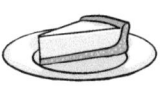

cake

قاطو

egg

بيض

fried egg

بيض مقلي

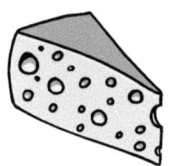

cheese

فرماج

ice cream

لاكرام

sugar

سكر

honey

عسل

jam

كونفتير

chocolate spread

نوقا

curry

الكاري

farm
فيرما

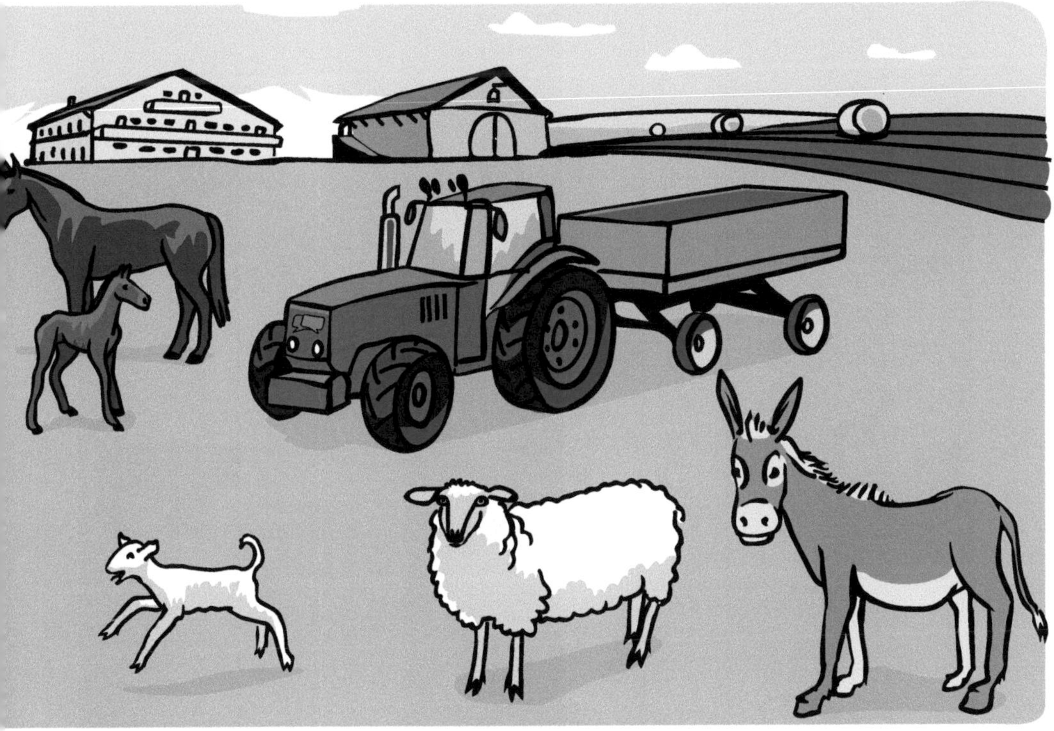

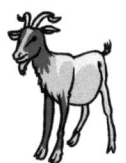

goat

معزة

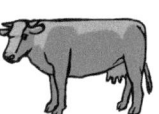

cow

بقرة

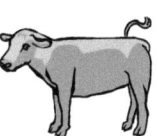

calf

عجل

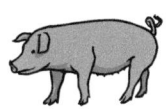

pig

حلوف

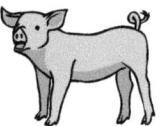

piglet

حلوف صغير

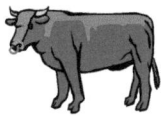

bull

طورو

goose

وزة

duck

بطة

chick

فلوس

hen

جاجة

cock

سردوك

rat

طوبا

cat

قطة

mouse

فأر

ox

ثور

dog

كلب

doghouse

دار الكلب

garden hose

تيبو

watering can

إبريق

scythe

منجل

plough

محراث

sickle

منجل

hoe

الفاس

pitchfork

مذراة الزبل

axe

شاقور

wheelbarrow

برويطة

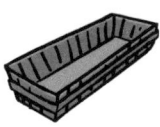

trough

معلف

milk can

قابة تاع حليب

sack

ساشيا

fence

سياج

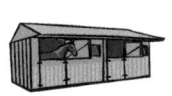

stable

صطبل

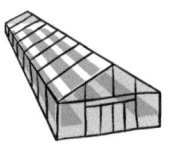

greenhouse

بوطاجي

soil

تراب

seed

بذور

fertilizer

سماد

combine harvester

حصادة

harvest

يحصد

harvest

الغلة

yams

بطاط

wheat

قمح

soy

صويا

potato

بطاطا

corn

مابيس

rapeseed

سلجم

fruit tree

شجرة تاع فاكية

cassava

منيهوت

cereals

الخبوب

house

دار

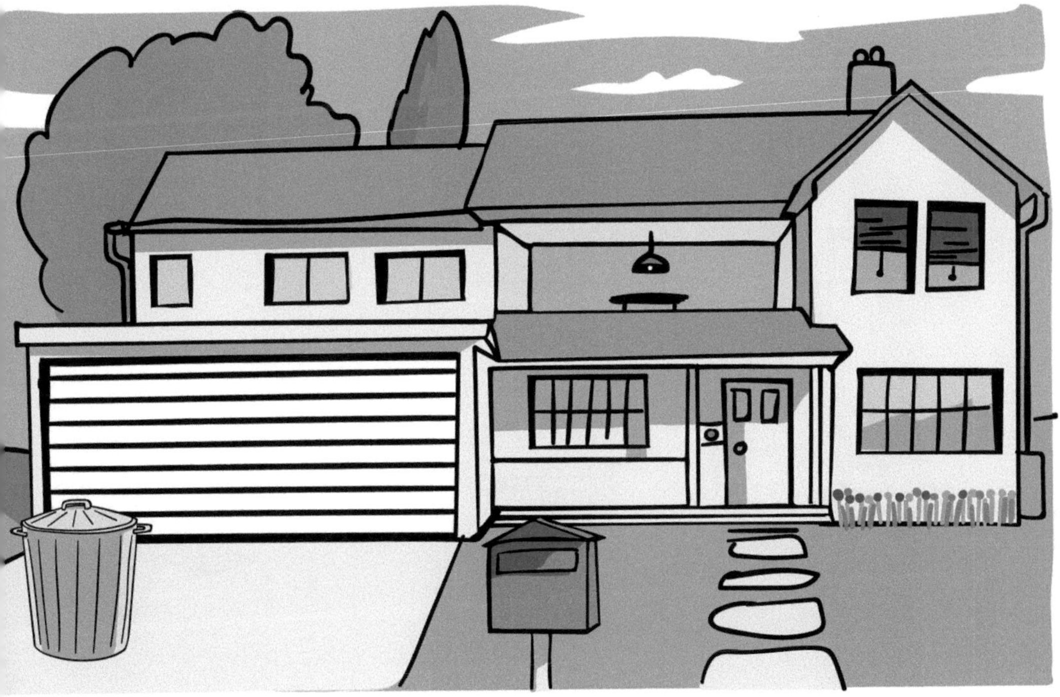

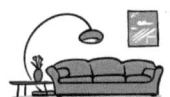

living room

صالون

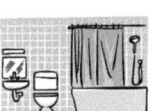

bathroom

الحمام

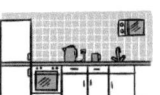

kitchen

كوزينا

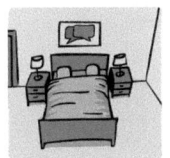

bedroom

شامبرا تاع رقاد

child's room

شمبرا تاع ذراري

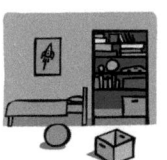

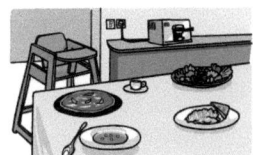

dining room

صالة مونجي

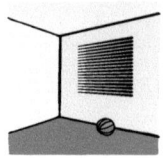

floor

لرض

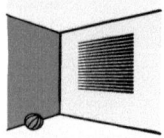

wall

حيط

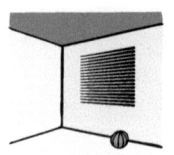

ceiling

وفالب

cellar

كافا

sauna

سونا

balcony

بالكون

terrace

تيراسة

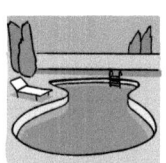

pool

بيسين

lawn mower

جزارة تاع حشيش

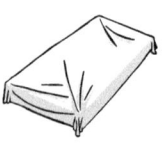

sheet

اووس

bedspread

كووات

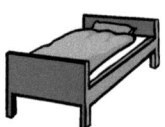

bed

ناموسية

broom

مصلحة

bucket

بيدو تاع صليح

switch

انتغيتور

living room
صالون

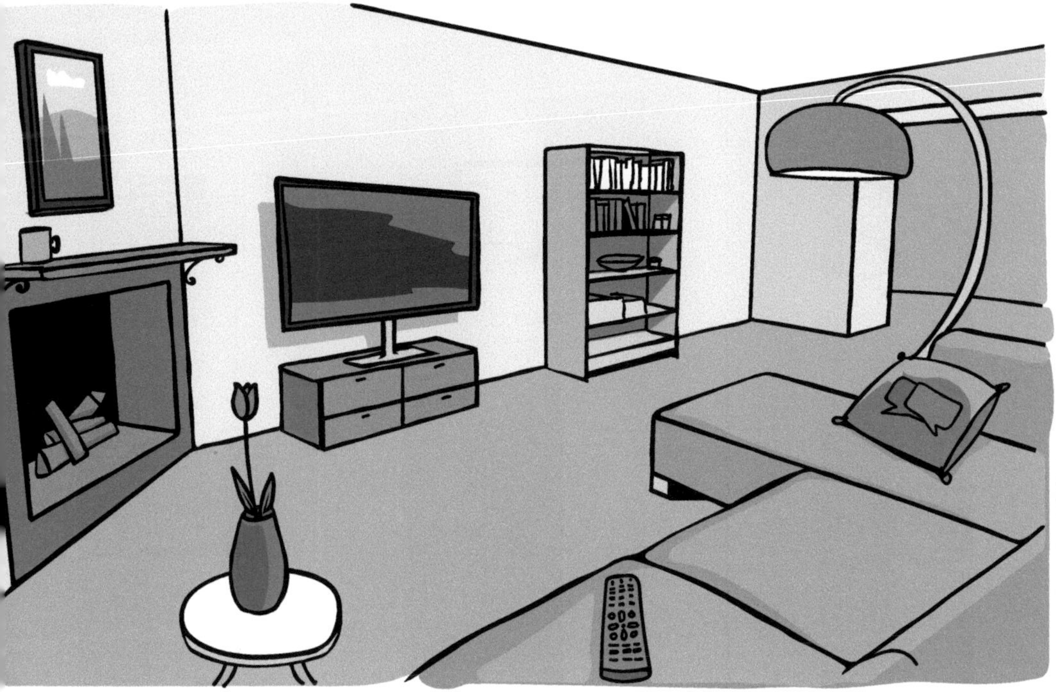

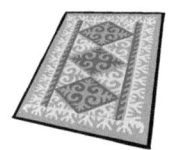

carpet

....

طابي

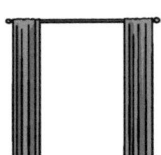

curtain

....

ريدو

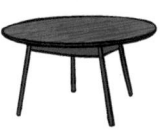

table

....

طابلة

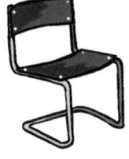

chair

....

كرسي

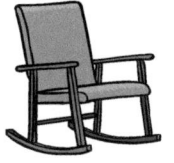

rocking chair

....

كرسي يبوجي

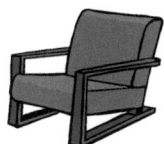

armchair

....

فوتاي

book

كتاب

blanket

طوفيرطة

decoration

زواق

firewood

الحطب

film

فيلم

hi-fi equipment

الستيريو

key

مفتاح

newspaper

جرنان

painting

كادر

poster

بوستار

radio

راديو

notepad

كناش

hoover

اسبيراتور

cactus

صبار

candle

شمعة

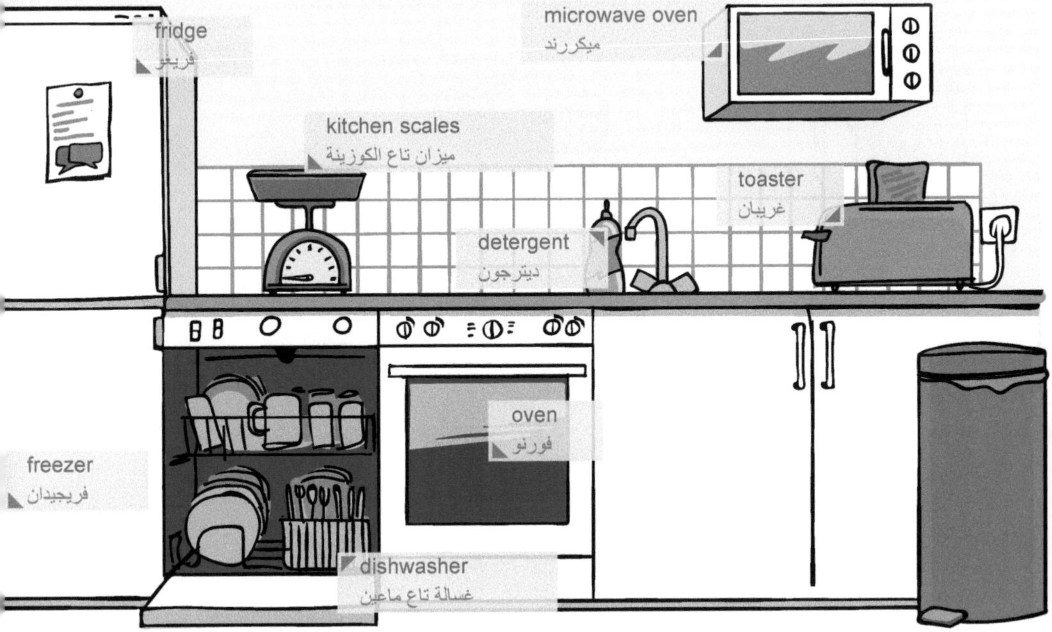

fridge
فريجو

microwave oven
ميكرند

kitchen scales
ميزان تاع الكوزينة

toaster
غريبان

detergent
ديترجون

oven
فورنو

freezer
فريجيدان

dishwasher
غسالة تاع ماعين

cooker

الفور

pot

قدرة

cast-iron pot

مرميطا

wok / kadai

طاوة غامقة

pan

مقلة

kettle

غلاية

steamer

قدرة

baking tray

سني

crockery

ماعين

mug

قوبلي

bowl

طبسي

chopsticks

مطارق تاع الماكلة

ladle

لوشة

spatula

سباتولة

whisk

الضرابة

strainer

كسكاس

sieve

صفاية

grater

راب

mortar

مهراز

barbecue

شواية

open fire

موقد

chopping board

بلونشا

rolling pin

رولو

corkscrew

الحلال

can

قابسة

can opener

الحلال

pot holder

كتان

sink

لافابو

brush

بروسة

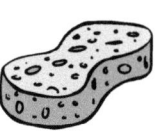

sponge

بونجة

blender

الخلاط

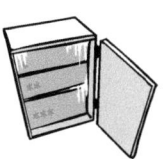

deep freezer

فريغو

baby bottle

بيبرونة

tap

سبالة

bathroom

الحمام

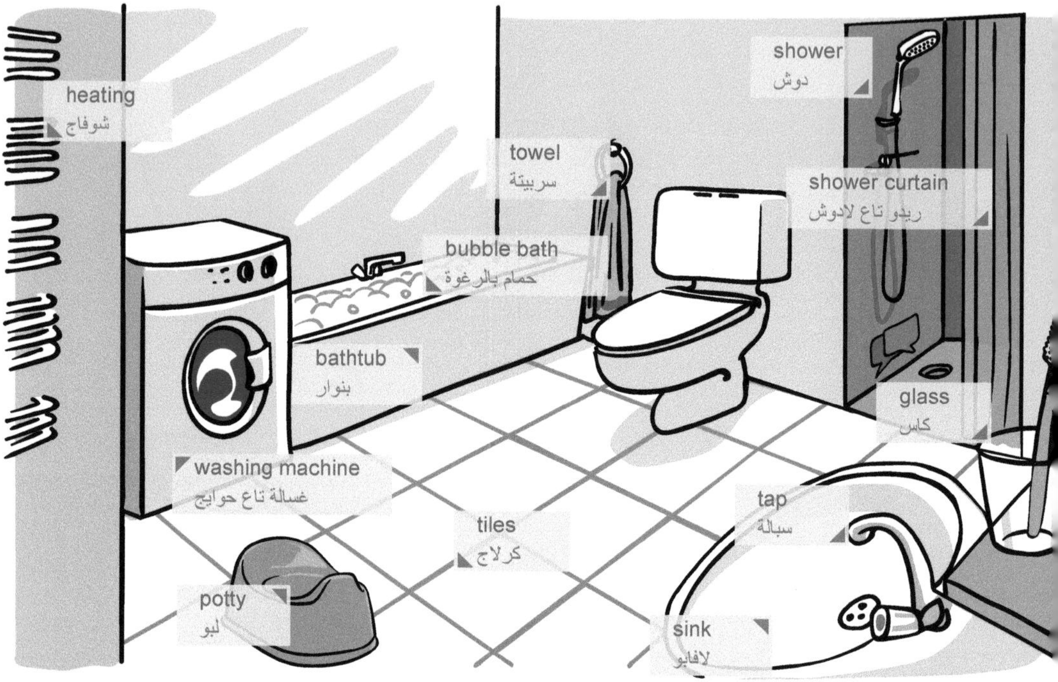

heating
شوفاج
towel
سربيتة
shower
دوش
shower curtain
ريدو تاع لادوش
bubble bath
حمام بالرغوة
bathtub
بنوار
glass
كاس
washing machine
غسالة تاع حوايج
tap
سبالة
tiles
كرلاج
potty
لبو
sink
لافابو

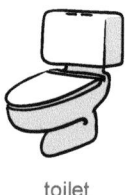

toilet

توالات

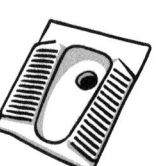

squat toilet

توالات تركي

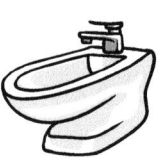

bidet

غسال الرجلين

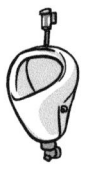

urinal

مبولة

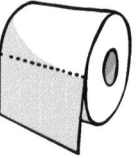

toilet paper

ورق تاع توالات

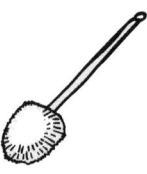

toilet brush

بروسة تاع توالات

toothbrush

بروسدون

toothpaste

دونتفريس

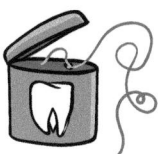

dental floss

خيط السنان

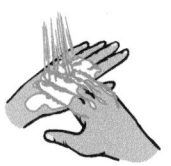

wash

يغسل

handheld shower

دوشات تاع دوش

douche

دوشات

basin

لافابو

back brush

بروسا تاع الظهر

soap

صابون

shower gel

شاو جال

shampoo

شنبوان

flannel

الحبل

drain

قادوس

cream

بومادة

deodorant

ديودورون

mirror

مراية

hand mirror

مراة صغيرة

razor

رازوار

shaving foam

لاموس

aftershave

كولون

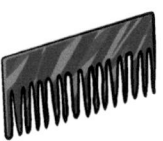

comb

مشطة

brush

بروسة

hair dryer

سشوار

hairspray

مثبت الشعر

makeup

مكياج

lipstick

روجالافر

nail varnish

فرني

cotton wool

قطن

nail scissors

كوبنغل

perfume

ريحة

washbag

تروسة تاع حمام

stool

طابوري

weighing scale

ميزان

bathrobe

بينوار

rubber gloves

ليغونات تاع النيتوياج

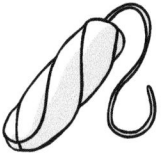

tampon

تمبون

sanitary towel

ليبوند

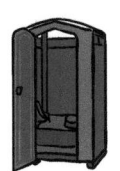

chemical toilet

توالات

child's room
شمبرا تاع ذراري

alarm clock
ريفاي
cuddly toy
نونورس
toy car
لوطو جوي
rattle
الخشخاش
doll's house
دار تاع بوبيات
present
كادو

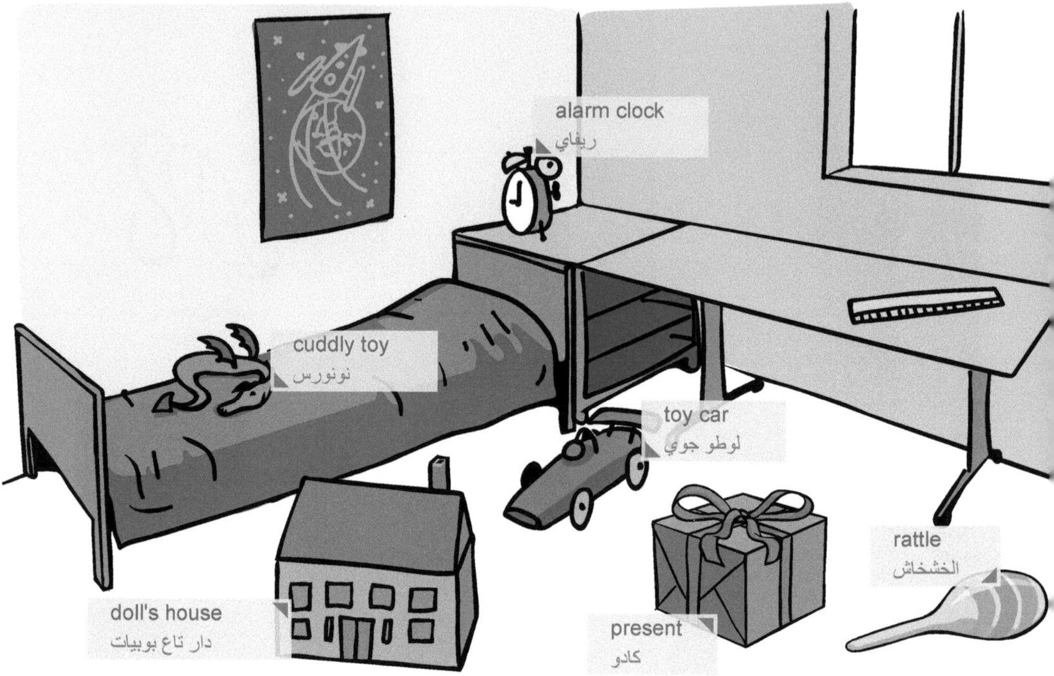

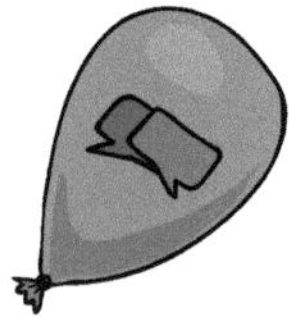

balloon

بالونة / نسافة

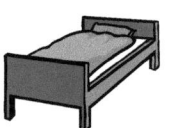

bed

ناموسية

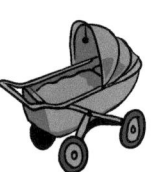

pram

بوسات

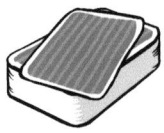

deck of cards

الكارطة

jigsaw

البوزيل

SUPER MEGA

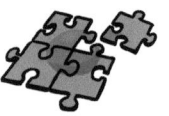

comic

بوند ديسيني

lego bricks

الليغو

building blocks

حجر يبنوه

action figure

بوبية

babygrow

لبسة تاع البيبي

frisbee

فريزي

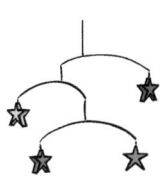

mobile

اللهاية

board game

لعبة الطابلة

dice

الدي

model train set

التران

dummy

سوسات

party

حفلة / الفيشطة

picture book

كتاب بتصاوير

ball

بالون

doll

بوبية

play

يلعب

sandpit

بارك بالرملة

swing

بنصوار

toys

جوي

video game console

منيطا

tricycle

بيسكلات

teddy bear

دبدوب

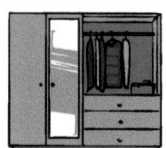

wardrobe

ماريو

clothing

حوايج

socks

تقاشر

stockings

ليبا

tights

كولو

scarf
شال

umbrella
بريلوي

t-shirt
تريكو

belt
حزام

boots
بوط

slippers
بنتوفلا

trainers
تينيسا / سبردينا

sandals	shoes	rubber boots
صندالة	صباط	بوط بلاستيك
underpants	bra	vest
كالسون	سوتيان	حويج تاع داخل

clothing - حوايج

body

لاصق على الجسم

trousers

سروال

jeans

جين

skirt

جيبا

blouse

طابلية

shirt

قمجة

pullover

تريكو

hoodie

قارديقون

blazer

بلازار

jacket

فيستا

coat

بالطو

raincoat

بالطو

costume

كوستيم

dress

روبا

wedding dress

روب بلونش

suit

كوستيم

nightgown

شوميز دونوي

pyjamas

بيجاما

sari

ساري

headscarf

حجاب

turban

عمامة

burqa

برقع

kaftan

قفطان

abaya

عباية

swimsuit

مايو

trunks

سروال تاع عوم

shorts

شورت

tracksuit

لبسة تاع سبور

apron

طابلية

gloves

ليقونات

button

قفلة

glasses

نواظر

bracelet

براسلي

necklace

سنسلة

ring

خاتم

earring

منقوش

cap

بوني

coat hanger

سانتر

hat

شابو

tie

قرافاطة

zip

غيمة

helmet

كاسك

braces

بروتال

school uniform

اللبة تاع ليكول

uniform

لينيفورم

bib

رياقة

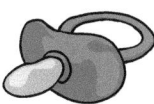

dummy

سوسات

nappy

شوكيل

server

سارفر

filing cabinet

خزانة تاع الملفات

printer

امبريمانت

paper

ورقة

monitor

ليكرون

mouse

لاسوري

desk

بيرو

folder

كلاسور

keyboard

كلافيي

waste-paper basket

بوبال

chair

كرسي

computer

اورديناتور

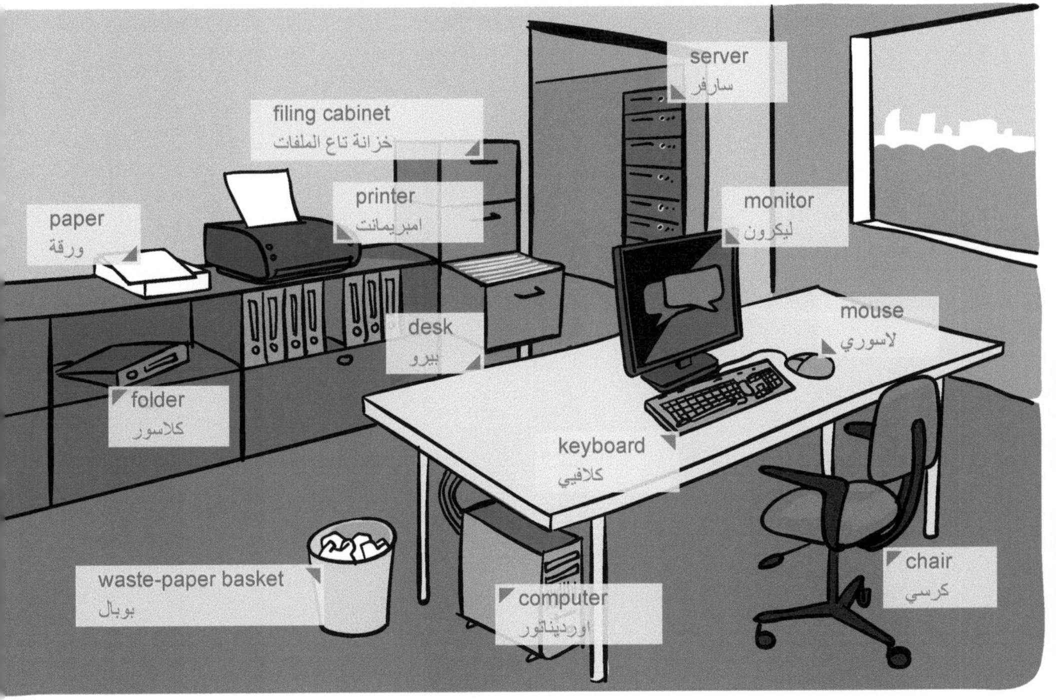

coffee mug

كاس قهوة

calculator

كاكولاتريس

internet

لانترنت

بيرو - office   49

laptop

أورديناتور

letter

برية

message

ميساج

mobile

بورطابل

network

ريزو

photocopier

فوطوكوبي

software

لوجسيال

telephone

تيلفون

plug socket

بريزة

fax machine

فاكس

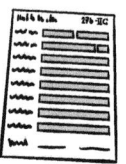

form

استمارة

document

وثيقة

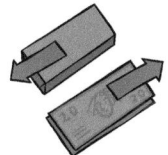

buy

يشري

pay

يخلص

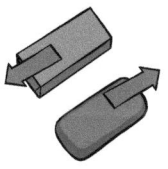

trade

يتاجر

money

دراهم

 **USD**

dollar

دولار

 **EUR**

euro

اورو

 **JPY**

yen

ين

 **RUB**

rouble

روبل

 **CHF**

Swiss franc

فرنك سويسري

 **CNY**

renminbi yuan

يوان

 **INR**

rupee

روبية

cashpoint

ديسترييبيتور

bureau de change

بيرة تاع الصرف

gold

ذهب

silver

فضة

oil

نفط

energy

طاقة

price

السومة

contract

عقد

tax

طاكس

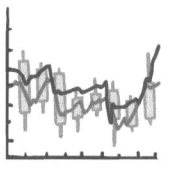

stock

سهم

work

يخدم

employee

خدام

employer

مول الشي

factory

وزين

shop

حانوت

police officer
بوليسي

fireman
بومبي

pilot
بيلوط

doctor
الطبيب

cook
طباخ

gardener

جرديني

carpenter

نجار

seamstress

خياط

judge

قاضي

chemist

شيميك

actor

ممثّل

bus driver

شوفير

taxi driver

طاكسيور

fisherman

صياد

cleaning lady

خدامة

roofer

ماصو تاع الصقف

waiter

سارفور

hunter

صياد

painter

بنتار

baker

خباز

electrician

الكتريسيان

builder

ماصون

engineer

مهندس

butcher

بوشي

plumber

بلومبي

postman

فاكتور

soldier

جندي

architect

ارشيتكت

cashier

كاسسي

florist

بياع اورد

hairdresser

كوافير

conductor

الكنترول

mechanic

ميكانيسيان

captain

كابيتان

dentist

طبيب سنان

scientist

عالم

rabbi

حاخام

imam

امام

monk

موان

clergyman

موان

tools
ليزوتي

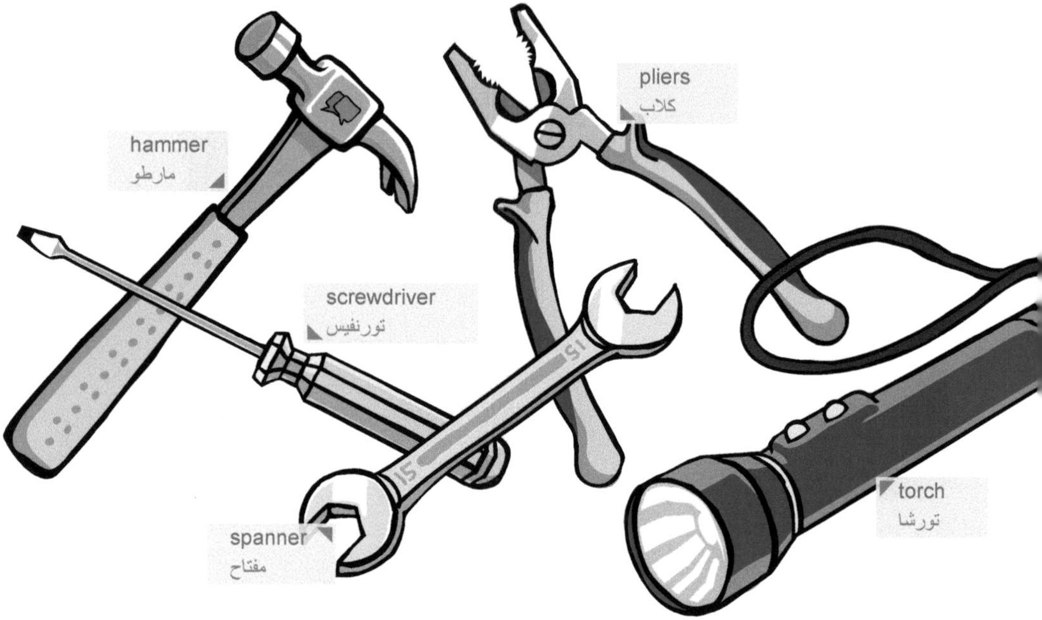
hammer
مارطو
pliers
كلاب
screwdriver
تورنفيس
spanner
مفتاح
torch
تورشا

digger

جرافة

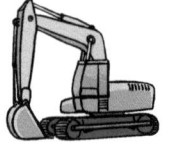

toolbox

قايصة نتاع ليزوتي

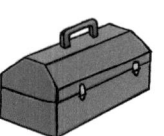

ladder

سلوم

saw

منشار

nails

مسامير

drill

برسوز

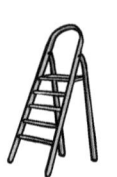

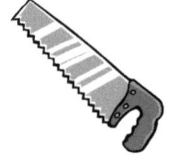

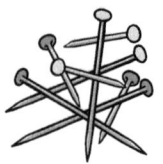

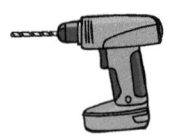

repair

يصنع

shovel

البالة

Damn!

ياويلي

dustpan

بالا

paint pot

بو تاع بنتورة

screws

ليفيس

musical instruments

آلات موسيقية

loudspeaker
مكبر الصوت

drum kit
آلات الإيقاع

guitar
غيتارة

▼ double bass
كمان أجهر

trumpet
بوق

piano

بيانو

violin

كمنجة

bass

جهير

timpani

طبل كبير

drums

طبل

keyboard

بيانو كهربائي

saxophone

ساكسوفون

flute

ناي

microphone

ميكروفون

حديقة حيوانات

entrance
المدخلة

tiger
نمر

cage
كاجا

zebra
حمار الوحش

animal feed
علف للحيوانات

panda
باندا

animals

حيوانات

elephant

فيل

kangaroo

كنغر

rhino

وحيد القرن

gorilla

غوريلا

bear

دب

camel

جمل

ostrich

نعامة

lion

سبع

monkey

تشيطا

flamingo

فلامونغوز

parrot

بيروكي

polar bear

دب قطبي

penguin

بطريق

shark

سمك القرش

peacock

طاووس

snake

لفعة

crocodile

تمساح

zookeeper

عساس في حديقة الحيوان

seal

عجل البحر

jaguar

نمر أمريكي مرقط

pony

فرس قزم

leopard

نمر

hippo

فرس النهر

giraffe

زرافة

eagle

نسر

boar

حلوف

fish

حوت

turtle

فكرون

walrus

حيوان فظ البحري

fox

ثعلب

gazelle

غزال

American football
بالون اميريكا

cycling
الركبة تاع البيسكلت

tennis
تينيس

basketball
باسكات

swimming
العوم

boxing
بوكس

ice hockey
هوكي

football

بالون

badminton

الريشة الطائرة

athletics

اتلاتيزم

handball

الهوند

skiing

سكي

polo

بولو

jump
ينقز

laugh
يضحك

hug
يعنق

walk
يمشي

sing
يغني

dream
ينوم

pray
يصلي

kiss
يبوس

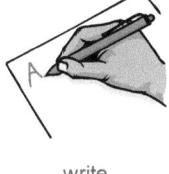

write
يكتب

draw
يرسم

show
يوري

push
يدمر

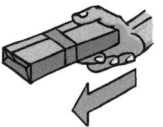

give
يعطي

take
يدي

have

يملك

do

يخدم

be

كاين

stand

يوقف

run

يجري

pull

يجبد

throw

يقيس / يرمي

fall

يطيح

lie

يتكسل

wait

يشوف

carry

يرفد

sit

يقعد

get dressed

يلبس

sleep

يرقد

wake up

ينوظ

look at

يشوف في

cry

يبكي

stroke

يحك

comb

يمشّط

talk

يهدر

understand

يفهم

ask

يسقسي

listen

يسمع

drink

يشرب

eat

ياكل

tidy up

يخمل

love

يبغي

cook

يطيب

drive

يصوق

fly

يطير

sail

يبحر بالفلوكة

calculate

يحسب

read

يقرا

learn

يتّعلم

work

يخدم

marry

يتزوج

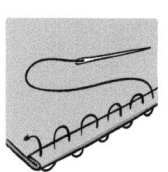

sew

يخيط

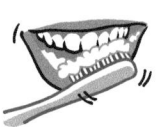

brush teeth

يغسل سنانو

kill

يكتل

smoke

يكمي

send

يرسل

family
لعايلة

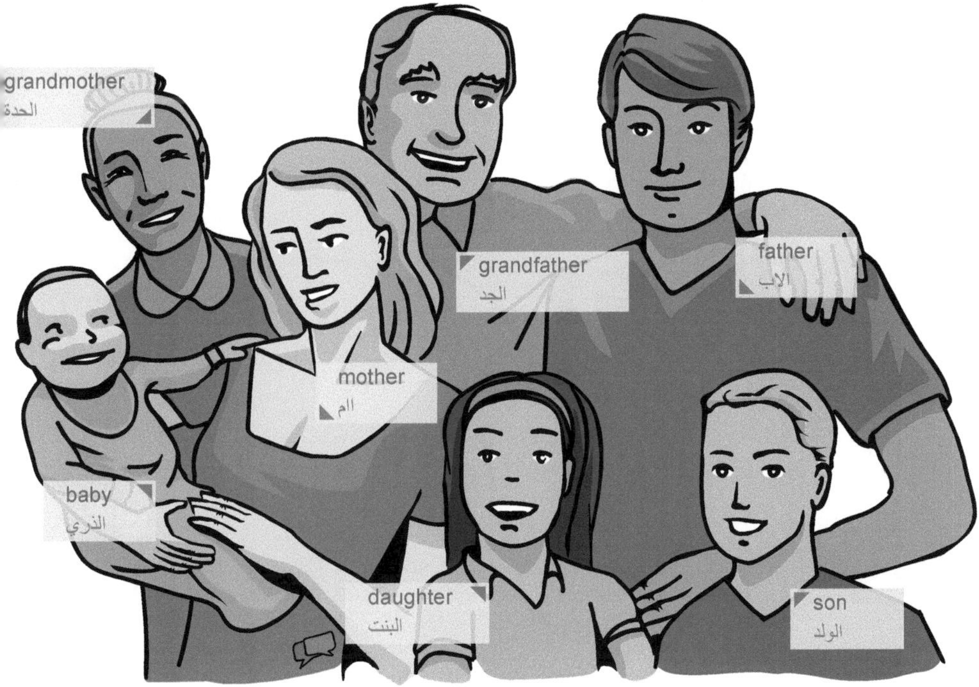
grandmother
الجدة
grandfather
الجد
father
الاب
mother
ام
baby
الذري
daughter
البنت
son
الولد

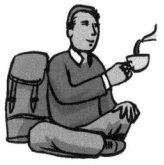

guest

ضيف

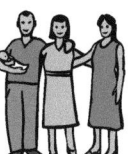

aunt

العمة / الخالة

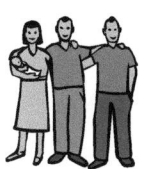

uncle

العم / الخال

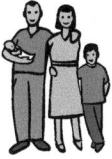

brother

الخو

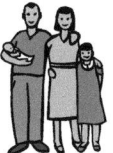

sister

الخت

body

الجسم

forehead
الجبهة
eye
العين
shoulder
الكتف
finger
صبع
face
الوجه
chin
اللحية
hand
اليد
breast
الصدر
leg
الساق
arm
الذراع

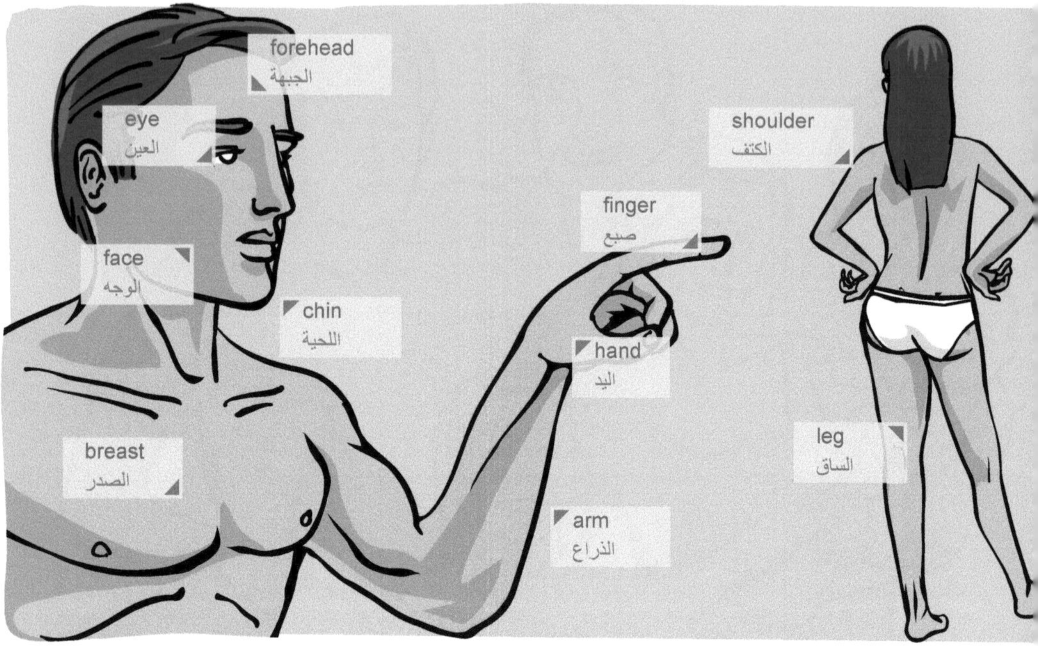

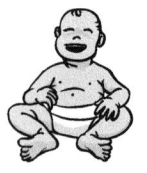

baby

الذري

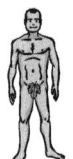

man

الراجل

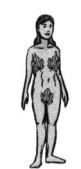

woman

المرا

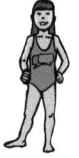

girl

الشيرة، الطفلة

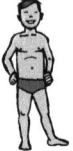

boy

الشير

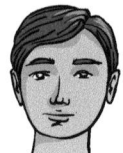

head

الراس

back

ظهر

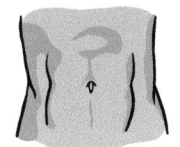

belly

الكرش

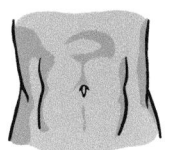

belly button

السرة

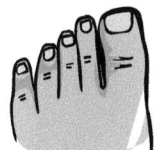

toe

صبع

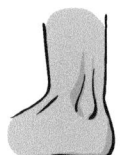

heel

طالون

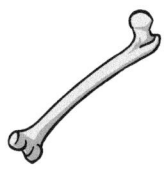

bone

العظم

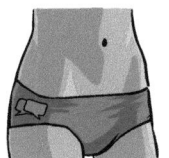

hip

المرادف

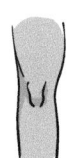

knee

الركبة

elbow

لمرفغ

nose

نيف

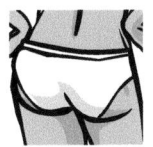

bottom

مصاصيط

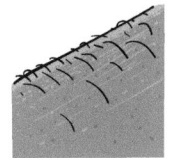

skin

البشرة

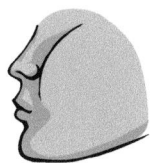

cheek

الحنوك

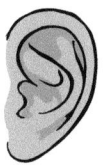

ear

لوذن

lip

شورب

mouth

الفم

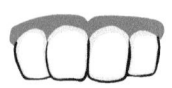

tooth

السنة

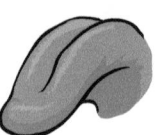

tongue

اللسان

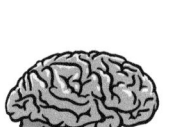

brain

الدماغ

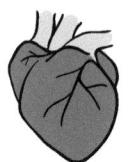

heart

القلب

muscle

العضلة

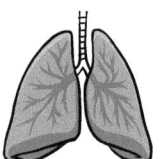

lung

الرية

liver

الكبدة

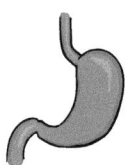

stomach

لسطوما

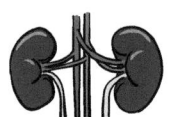

kidneys

كلوى

sex

رابور

condom

بريزارفتيف

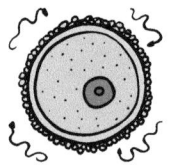

ovum

البويضة

semen

سبرم

pregnancy

بلكرش

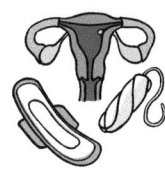

menstruation

ليراغل

vagina

المهبل

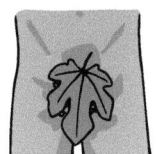

penis

المذاكر

eyebrow

الحاجب

hair

الشعر

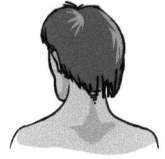

neck

رقبة

hospital
سبيطار

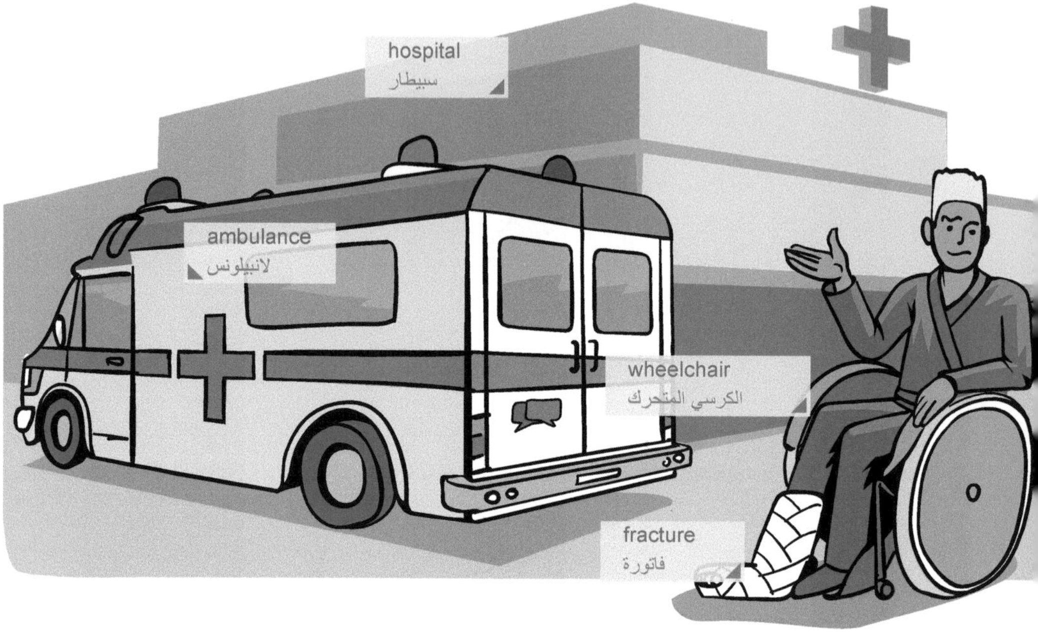

hospital
سبيطار
ambulance
لانبيلونس
wheelchair
الكرسي المتحرك
fracture
فاتورة

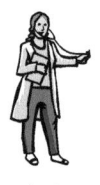

doctor
الطبيب

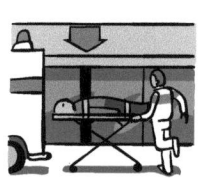

emergency room
ليزيرجونس

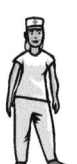

nurse
الممرضة

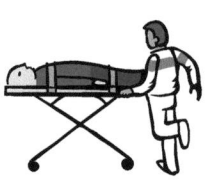

emergency
ليرجونس

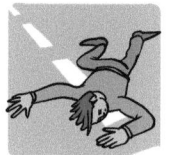

unconscious
تغاشى

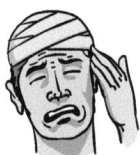

pain
الوجع

injury

الجرح

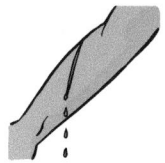

bleeding

يسل الدم

heart attack

القلب

stroke

لافيسي

allergy

لالرجي

cough

الكحة

fever

الحمة

flu

لاقريب

diarrhoea

الاسهال

headache

ميغران

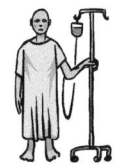

cancer

السرطان

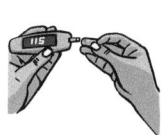

diabetes

السكر

surgeon

الجراح

scalpel

مبضع

operation

عملية تاع القلب

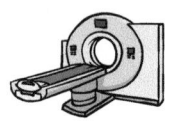

CT

لاسيتي

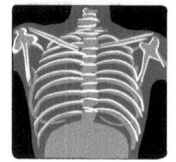

x-ray

الراديو

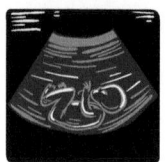

ultrasound

لولتخازرون

face mask

لماسك

disease

المرض

waiting room

وين يقارعو

crutch

العكاز

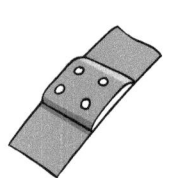

plaster

سكوتش

bandage

لبانسما

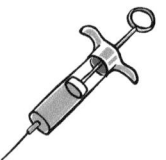

injection

لبرة

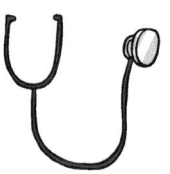

stethoscope

السماعة تاع الطبيب

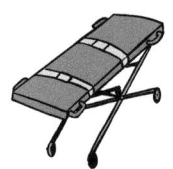

stretcher

نقالة

clinical thermometer

لوزنو بيه الحمة

birth

زيادة

overweight

السمونية

hearing aid

جهاز السمع

disinfectant

المعقم

infection

لنفكسون

virus

الفيروس

HIV / AIDS

السيدا

medicine

الدوا

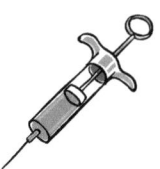

vaccination

الفاكسان

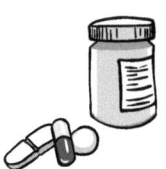

tablets

الدوا حب

pill

بيلولة

emergency call

يِعيط للنجدة

blood pressure monitor

الجهاز ليقيسو بيه الدم

ill / healthy

مريض / صحيح

Help! سلكوني	 alarm لالارم	 assault يتعدا
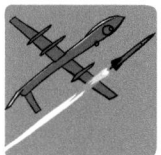 attack يهجم	 danger دونجي	 emergency exit مخرج الطوارى
Fire! النار شاعلة	 fire extinguisher لكستانتور	 accident اكسيدون
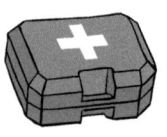 first-aid kit فيزة تاع الاسعاف الاولي	 SOS سلكونا	 police لابوليس

Europe

أوروبا

North America

أمريكا الشمالية

South America

أمريكا الجنوبية

Africa

أفريقيا

Asia

آسيا

Australia

أستراليا

Atlantic

المحيط الأطلسي

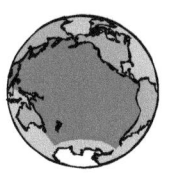

Pacific

المحيط الهادي

Indian Ocean

المحيط الهندي

Antarctic Ocean

المحيط المتجمد الجنوبي

Arctic Ocean

المحيط المتجمد الشمالي

North Pole

القطب الشمالي

South Pole
القطب الجنوبي

Antarctica
منطقة القطب الجنوبي

Earth
أرض

land
بلاد

sea
بحر

island
جزيرة

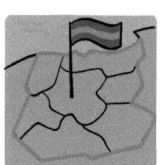

nation
امة

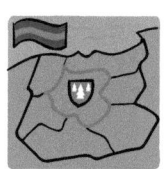

state
دولة

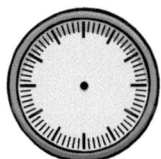

clock face

ميناء الساعة

hour hand

عقرب الساعات

minute hand

عقرب الدقائق

second hand

عقرب الثواني

What time is it?

شعال راها الساعة؟

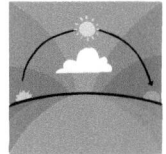

day

يوم

time

زمن

now

دروك

digital watch

ساعة رقمية

minute

دقيقة

hour

ساعة

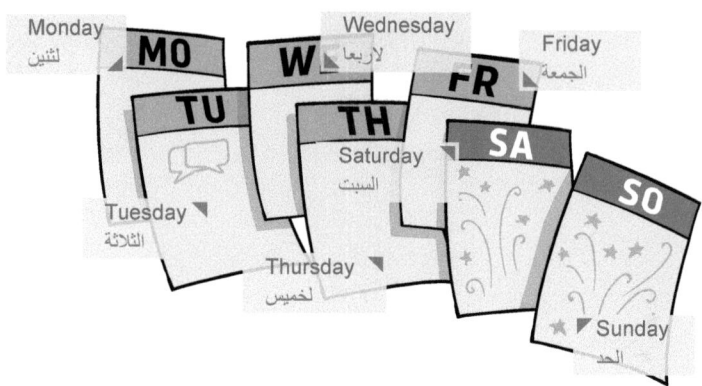

Monday
لثنين

Wednesday
لاريعا

Friday
الجمعة

Tuesday
الثلاثة

Saturday
السبت

Thursday
لخميس

Sunday
الحد

yesterday

لبارح

today

اليوم

tomorrow

غدوا

morning

صباح

noon

القايلة

evening

العشية

business days

يامات الخدمة

weekend

ويكاند

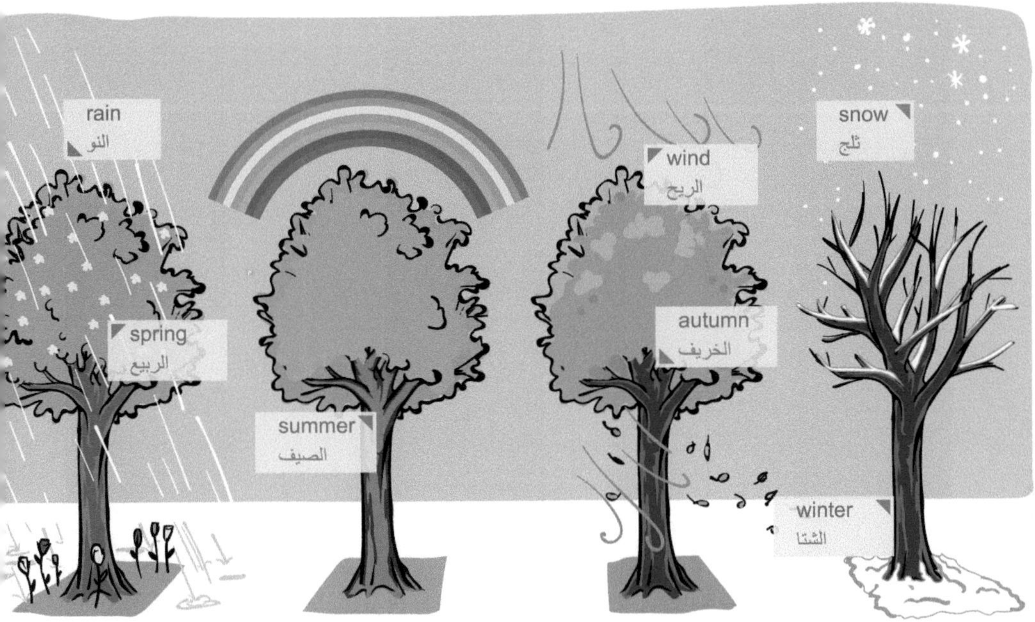

rain
النو
spring
الربيع
summer
الصيف
wind
الريح
autumn
الخريف
snow
ثلج
winter
الشتا

4.APRIL 11°
5.APRIL 4°
6.APRIL 13°
7.APRIL 8°
8.APRIL 10°

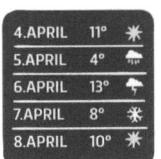

weather forecast

يتنبأ بالحال

F C
120 40
90 30
60 20
30 10
0 0
-30 -10
-20

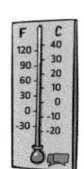

thermometer

مقياس حرارة

sunshine

ضوء الشمس

cloud

سحابة

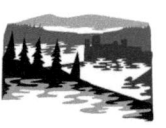

fog

ضباب

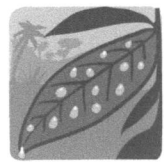

humidity

ميديتي

lightning

برق

thunder

رعد

storm

عاصفة

hail

بَرَد

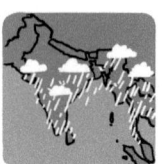

monsoon

ريح

flood

طوفان

ice

جليد

January

جانفي

February

فيفري

March

مارس

April

افريل

May

ماي

June

جوان

July

جويلية

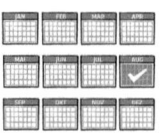

August

اوت

September

سبتمبر

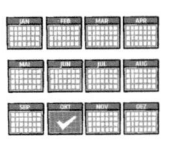

October

اكتوبر

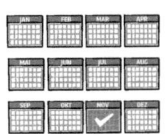

November

نوفمبر

December

ديسمبر

shapes

فورما

circle

دويرة

square

مربع

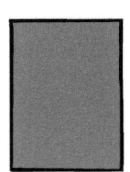

rectangle

مستطيل

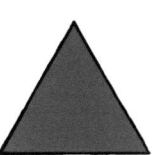

triangle

مثلث

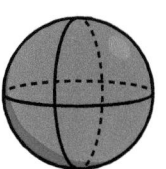

sphere

كويرة

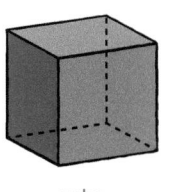

cube

مكعب

white

بيض

yellow

صفر

orange

تشيني

pink

روز

red

حمر

purple

حلحالي

blue

زرق

green

خظر

brown

قهوي

grey

قري

black

كحل

a lot / a little

بزاف / شوية

angry / calm

زعفان / مكالمي

beautiful / ugly

شباب / مشي شباب

beginning / end

البدية / التالي

big / small

كبير / صغير

bright / dark

فاتح / فونسي

brother / sister

خو / خت

clean / dirty

نقي / موسخ

complete / incomplete

كامل / ناقص

day / night

نهار / اليل

dead / alive

ميت / حي

wide / narrow

عريض / ضيق

edible / inedible

يقدر ياكله / ميقدرش ياكله

evil / kind

شرير / ناس ملاح

excited / bored

يثير / يمل

fat / thin

سمين / رقيق

first / last

اللولا / التالية

friend / enemy

الصاحب / لعدو

full / empty

معمر / فارغ

hard / soft

قاصح / سوبل

heavy / light

ثقيل / خفيف

hunger / thirst

جوع / عطش

ill / healthy

مريض / صحيح

illegal / legal

غير شرعي / شرعي

intelligent / stupid

ذكي / مبوقل

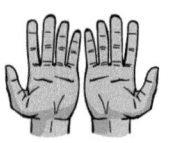

left / right

يسار / يمين

near / far

قريب / بعيد

new / used

جديد / مستعمل

nothing / something

مكانش / شوية

old / young

شيباني / شاب

on / off

يشعل / يطفئ

open / closed

محلول / مبلع

quiet / loud

بشوية / بلفور

rich / poor

مرفح / زوالي

right / wrong

نيشان / خاطيء

rough / smooth

حرش / رطب

sad / happy

زعفان / فرحان

short / long

قصير / طويل

slow / fast

بشوية / بلخف

wet / dry

مثمخغ / ناشف

warm / cool

حامي / بارد

war / peace

القيرة / لامان

0

zero

صفر

1

one

واجد

2

two

زوج

3

three

ثلاثة

4

four

ربعة

5

five

خمسة

6

six

ستة

7

seven

سبعة

8

eight

ثمانية

9

nine

تسعة

10

ten

عشرة

11

eleven

حداعش

12

twelve

ثناعش

13

thirteen

تلطاعش

14

fourteen

رباطاعش

15

fifteen

خمسطاعش

16

sixteen

سطاعش

17

seventeen

سبعطتعش

18

eighteen

ثمنطاعش

19

nineteen

تساعطاش

20

twenty

عشرون

100

hundred

مية

1.000

thousand

ألف

1.000.000

million

مليون

languages

English

انقلى

American English

انغلى تاع مريكان

Chinese Mandarin

لغة الشنوية

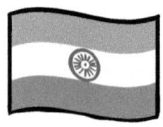

Hindi

الهندية

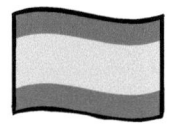

Spanish

سبينيولية

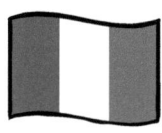

French

الفرونسي

Arabic

العربية

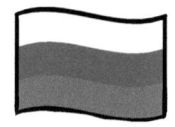

Russian

الروسية

Portuguese

البوتغالية

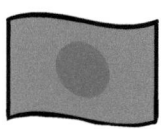

Bengali

البنغالية

German

لالمنية

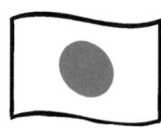

Japanese

الجابونية

I

انا

you

نتا

he / she / it

هو

we

حنايا

you

نتوما

they

هوما

who?

شكون

what?

واش

how?

كيفاش

where?

وين

when?

وقتاش

name

الاسم

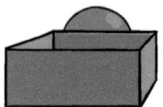

behind

مرول

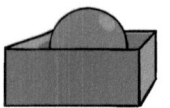

in

في

in front of

قدام

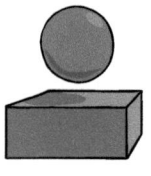

over

فوق

on

على

under

تحت

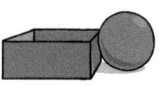

beside

حدا

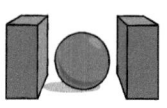

between

بين

place

بلاصة